Usborne
Pocket
Optical
illusions

Designed and illustrated by
Hanri Van Wyk and Matt Durber

Written by Sam Taplin

There's more information
about the illusions in the
answers section at the
back of the book.

Which of the three splashes of paint is exactly the same shade of blue as the one on the brush? Turn to the answers section at the back to find out.

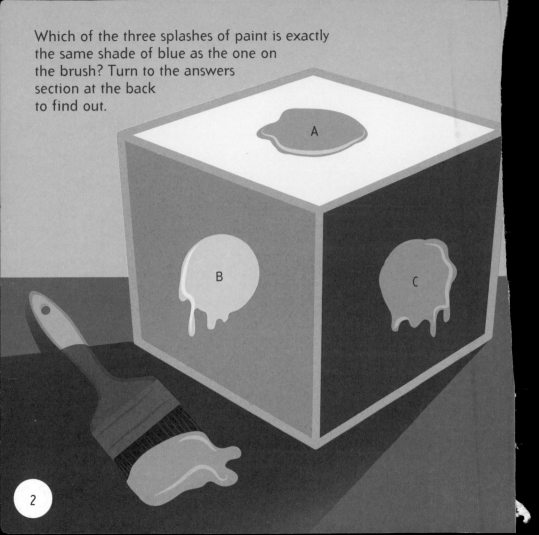

Are the squares in the middle of this board slightly wavy? Check them with a ruler, then look at the answers section.

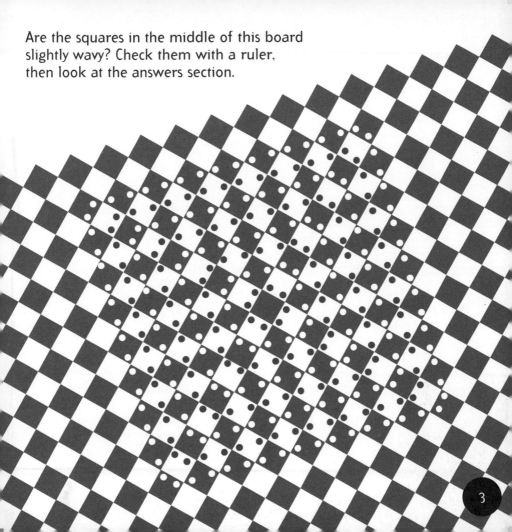

Do the black and white rings look like perfect circles, or are they squashed? The answers section will tell you.

4

Using a ruler, draw a straight line from the dot in the middle to each dot around the circle. Do the straight blue lines look as though they're tilting?

Can you see how the circle looks as though it's bulging out of the page? You can make the heart look 3-D as well, by drawing a curved line between each pair of straight ones. If your lines curve up, the heart will seem to bulge, and if your lines curve down, it will seem to sink into the page.

Are the red and yellow lines slanting and curving? Use a ruler to check, then see the answers to discover how this illusion works.

Shade the rest of the shapes in, following this pattern of orange, blue and yellow. Can you now see lots of cubes?

8

Are the orange shapes the top of the cubes, or the bottom? Can you see the cubes both ways? See the answers to find out how.

9

Look at the small blue triangles in the middle of these shapes. Triangle A is exactly the same shade as one of the others. But which one? Turn to the answers when you think you've figured it out.

Move your eyes around this arrow pattern.
Does it look as though the middle section of arrows
is slowly falling, and the other sections are rising?

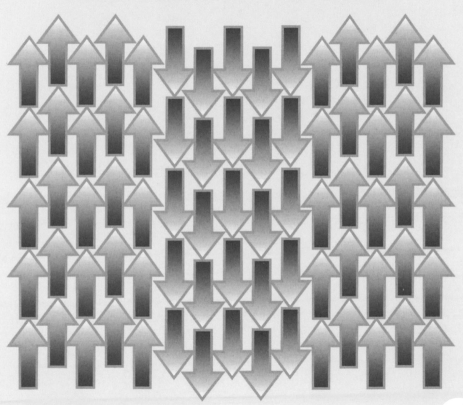

Use a ruler to draw a line between each pair of dots that have the same letter. Your lines will seem to be different lengths – but are they? Find out in the answers.

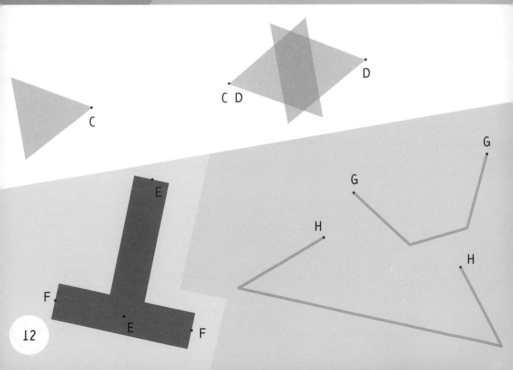

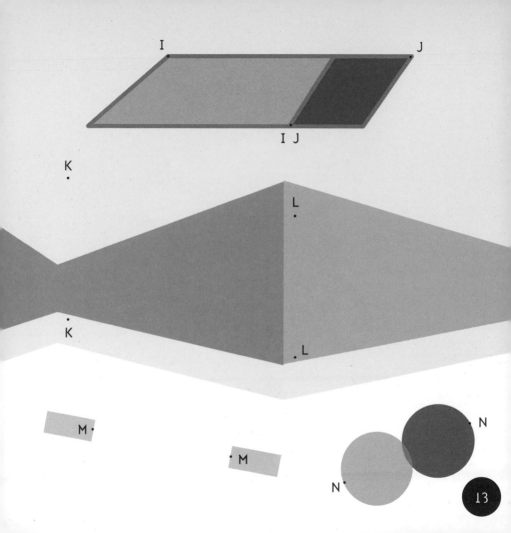

14

Using a black pen, give the monster on the opposite page eyes and a mouth. Then stare at the red X in the middle for at least 30 seconds. before looking into the white circle below. What happens?

Look at this pair of pictures.
Does one of the orange circles
look bigger than the other?

Pair 1

Now try this
pair. Does one of
the middle triangles
seem bigger?

Pair 2

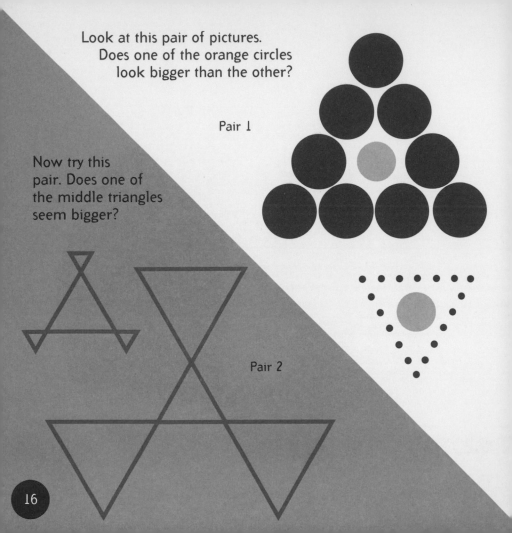

Which yellow hexagon seems bigger? Or are they the same?

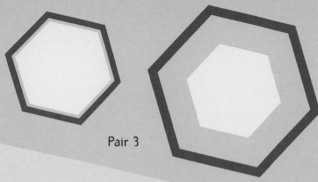

Pair 3

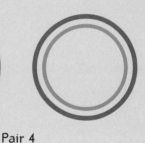

Pair 4

Does one of these blue circles look bigger?

Can you make these orange circles seem different by drawing more circles around them? See the answers for more about these illusions.

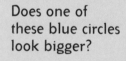

Pair 5

Move your eyes around this grid.
Can you see little pale dots
appearing and disappearing?
If you stare at any dot it will
vanish... but if you move
your eyes the dots will
appear again.

Stare at the black dot in the middle for at least 30 seconds.
What happens to the other dots? See the answers to find out more.

Fill in the dotted squares with black. Do the lines across the page look tilted now? The answers section has more about this illusion.

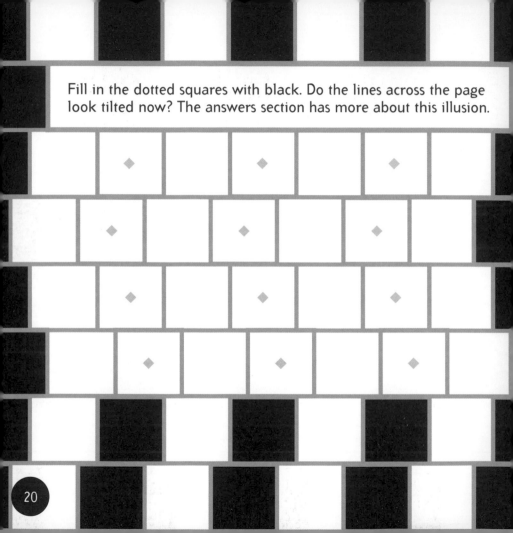

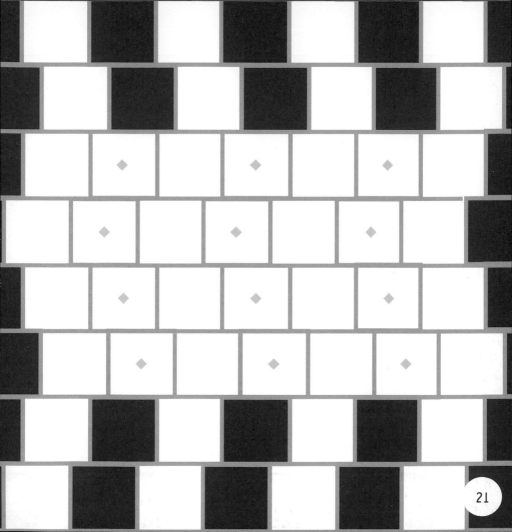

Do the two sets of orange stripes seem to be tilting at different angles? Use a ruler to check, then see the answers to find out.

Are the orange circles behind the stripes all slightly different shades? Find out the truth in the answers.

23

Move your eyes around this pattern. Can you see the circles spinning around? If you stare at one circle it will stay still... but the ones around it will start to move.

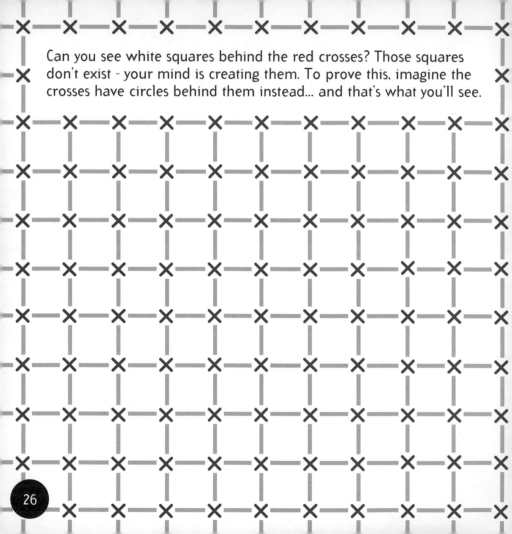

Can you see white squares behind the red crosses? Those squares don't exist - your mind is creating them. To prove this, imagine the crosses have circles behind them instead... and that's what you'll see.

Does the orange semi-circle on the left seem darker than the one on the right? Have a good look, then turn to the answers.

The two blue semi-circles also seem to be different shades. But are they really? The answers will tell you.

Join the dots to make a 3-D shape that you can see in two ways.
Is it a box in the corner of a room? Or one cube in front of another?

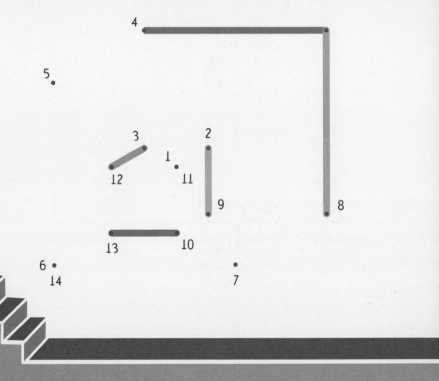

Here's another 3-D illusion that can be seen
in two different ways. Is it a flight of steps
seen from above... or from underneath?

Is this player kicking the ball towards you or away from you?
Can you see it both ways? See the answers to find out more.

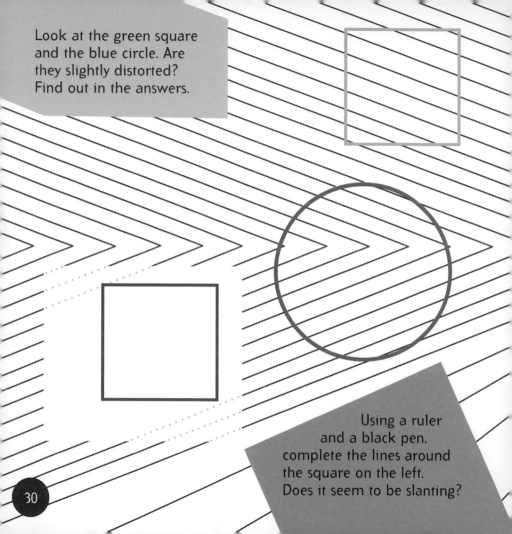

Look at the green square and the blue circle. Are they slightly distorted? Find out in the answers.

Using a ruler and a black pen, complete the lines around the square on the left. Does it seem to be slanting?

Are the sides of the purple square bending? Check them with a ruler, then turn to the answers.

Finish the black lines around the orange square, using a ruler. Do the sides of the square seem to be sloping?

31

Do some parts of this image seem closer to you than others?
Can you make yourself see the whole image as
one flat surface? Not easy, is it?

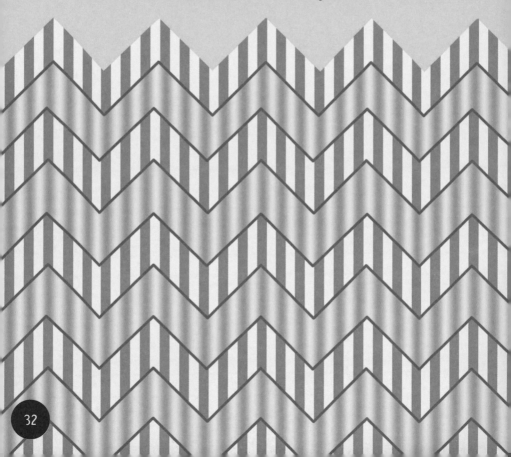

Move this page left and right. Is anything hidden among the stripes? Look at the answers to find out what's going on.

These three stripes
all seem to be
broken – the two
ends don't line up.
Or do they? Take
a good look, then
turn to the answers.

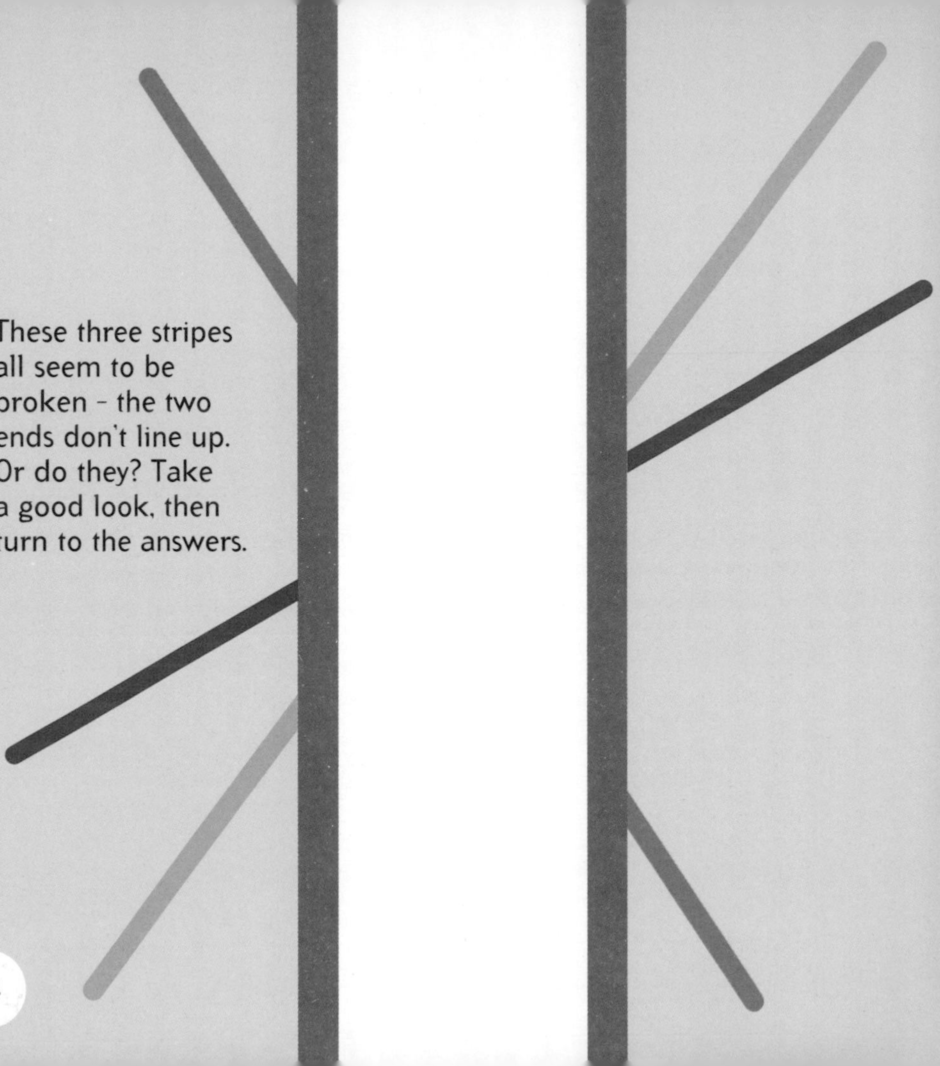

Draw a mirror image of the left-hand face on the right-hand side.
Then shade in the faces. Can you see a vase between them?
You can see more examples of this famous illusion at the bottom.

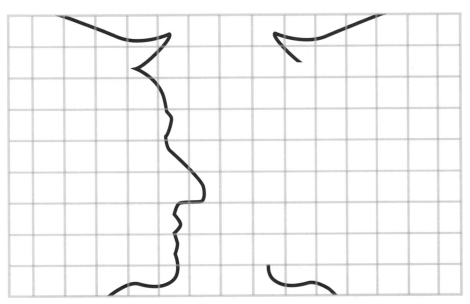

If you focus on the
vase, the faces are
the background.
If you stare at the
faces, it's the opposite.

Move your eyes around this grid. Can you see black dots appearing on top of the white ones? What happens if you try to stare directly at a black dot? (The answers will tell you more.)

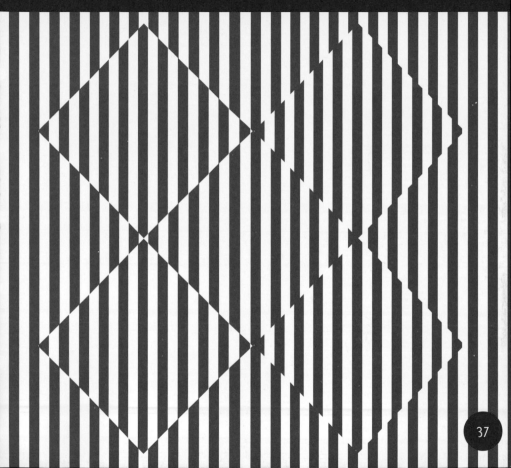

37

Is the yellow in stars A and B the same? Or is it brighter in one of them? Check the answers to find out.

A

B

C

D

Is star C lighter than star D? The answers will tell you what's happening.

Which of the circles is exactly halfway up the triangle? Try to answer without measuring, then check the answers to see if you were right.

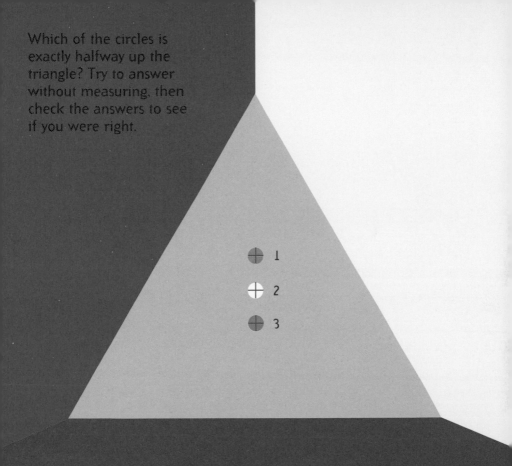

1

2

3

Look at the two triangles. Are the thin ends darker than the wide ones? Are you sure? Turn to the back of the book to find out.

Can you see little flashes sweeping up and down the yellow and orange lines? This happens because of the striped background. Using a black pen and a ruler, carefully add stripes behind the lines in the white box. Can you see the illusion on those lines as well now?

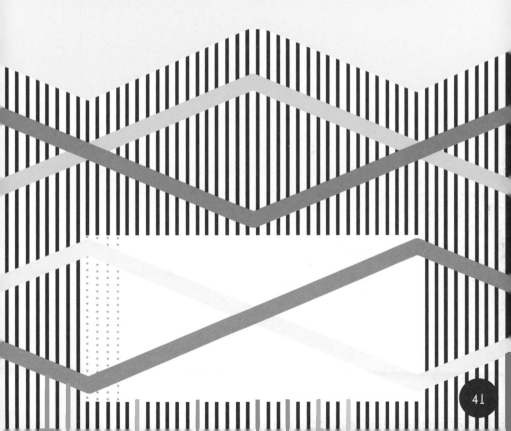

41

Stare at the black dot on this page for 30 seconds, then look inside the circle on the opposite page. What do you see?

43

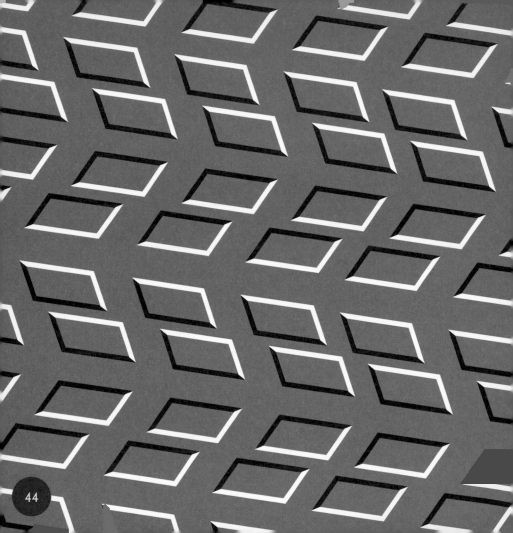

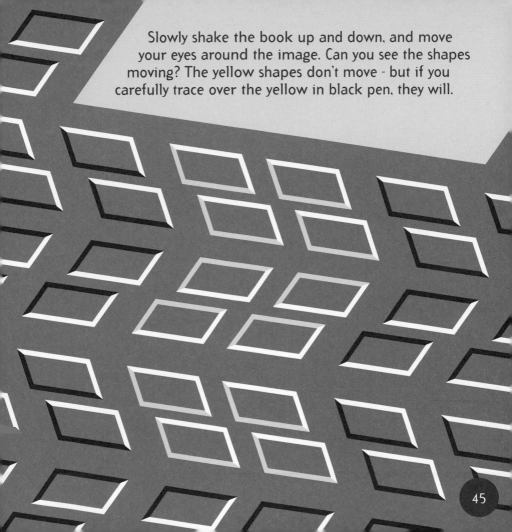

Slowly shake the book up and down, and move your eyes around the image. Can you see the shapes moving? The yellow shapes don't move - but if you carefully trace over the yellow in black pen, they will.

45

Can you see a diamond shape below? There's no diamond, but your mind creates it.

What yellow shape can you see here, in the middle of the circles?

Is there a green shape hiding among these circles?

Here you're looking at some white triangles on a red background. But can you see a red shape?

Fill in the shapes below to create your own version of this illusion.

Do these three blue shapes suggest a yellow shape to you?

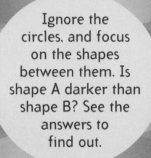

Ignore the circles, and focus on the shapes between them. Is shape A darker than shape B? See the answers to find out.

A

B

All these squares line
up with each other.
Carefully shade all the
white lines black. Does
the big square look as
though it's leaning and
distorted now?

Look at the two pairs of arrows. Do the "B" arrows look brighter than the "A" ones? Turn to the answers to find out what's going on here.

Prop the book open then walk across the room and look at this page from a distance. What happens to the picture? The answers will tell you more.

Move your eyes around this image. Do the arrows seem to be rotating? Shade the yellow areas black to make the illusion even stronger.

Can you work out how to turn these shapes into a normal picture? Once you've tried it, turn to the answers.

53

Can you understand the sentence below,
even with the letters jumbled?

Waht deos tihs snetence maen?

Read the sentence
on the right a
couple of times.
Is there anything
strange about it?

Can you find a a mistake in in this sentence?

54

It's quite easy to read this sentence even with the bottom half missing, isn't it?

But it's a little harder to read something when the top half has been taken away.

Can you read the two sentences above?

The answers will tell you more about all the illusions on these two pages.

Look at the blue balls. Is the one at the top slightly bigger than the one at the bottom? Trace over the two sets of dotted lines. You've drawn two more identical balls – but does the top one look bigger?

Is the pink background on
this page two different
shades? Are you sure?
See the answers to find out.

Do the long lines seem to be bending?
Finish off the little angled lines on the
opposite page, and the long lines
will seem to bend there too.

58

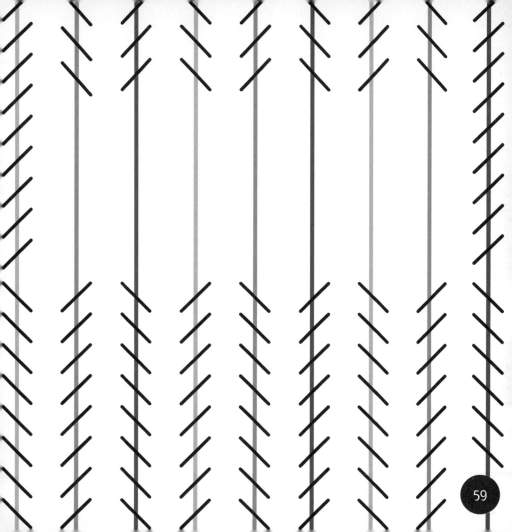

59

Stare at the X above for at least 30 seconds,
then stare at the X on the opposite page.

What happens when you look at this image?
Turn to the answers to find out more.

Take a quick look at the two smiling faces on these pages. (Don't turn the book upside down.)

Now turn the book upside down and take another look at this face. See the answers to find out what's going on.

These circles look squashed... but are they really? See the answers to find out.

64

Look at the diamond shape then shake the book gently from side to side. What happens? You can find out more in the answers section.

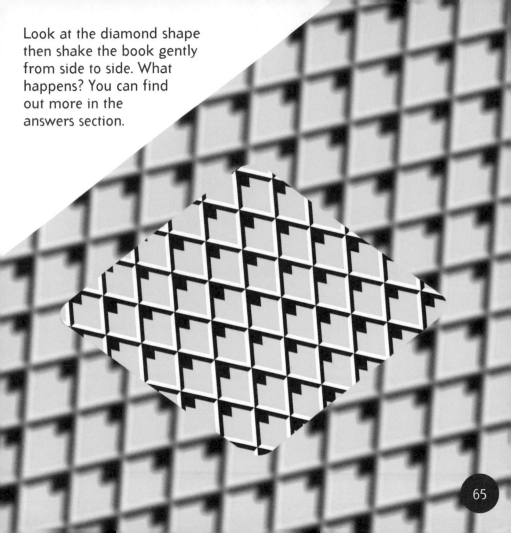

These two pairs of eyes seem to stare in different directions – but they're the same. The other pairs of faces also show this illusion.

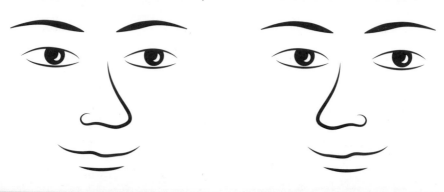

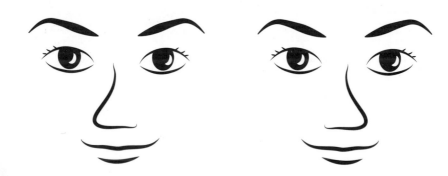

Here are two more sets of identical eyes. Can you copy the faces above to create your own version of the illusion?

The lollipop and candy canes seem to be tilting in different directions... but are they really? The answers will tell you.

You can create your own version of this illusion by finishing off the little lines in the image below.

Move your eyes around this image. Are you looking at one long spiral, or is it lots of separate circles? See the answers to find out.

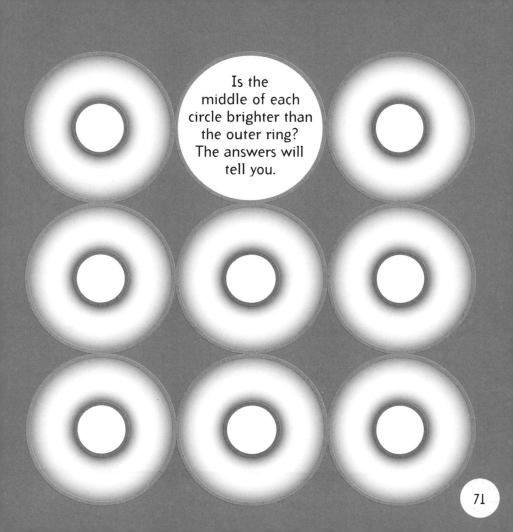

Is the middle of each circle brighter than the outer ring? The answers will tell you.

Do some of these lines look as though they're bending? Shade the yellow lines on the opposite page black to create the same illusion there.

72

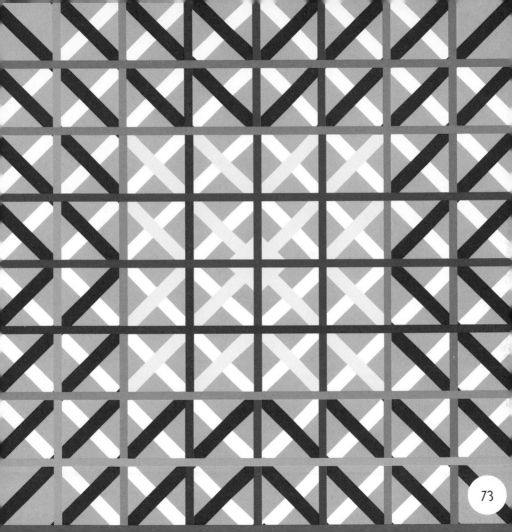

How many shades of red are there in this image? And how many shades of blue? How about yellow? Take a good look, then turn to the answers to find out.

Does this page seem to bulge upwards in a series of waves?

Trace carefully over the dots with a thick black pen
to create your own version of the illusion.

Which of these shapes is the biggest?
Guess without measuring, then turn to the answers.

Is the orange at the middle of this image brighter than the orange at the edges? The answers will tell you if it really is.

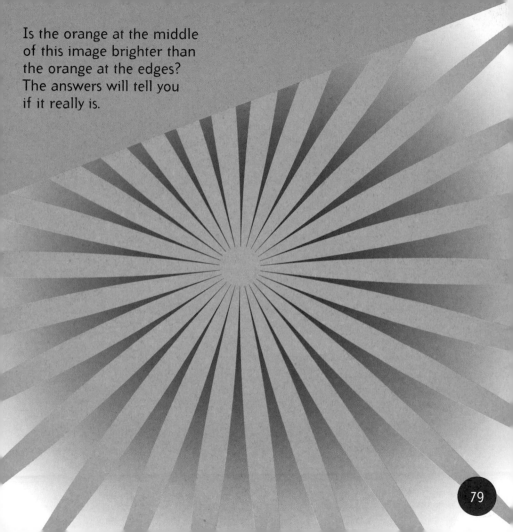

Look at the rows of circles going across these two pages. The rows are tilting, aren't they? Are you sure? Take a good look, then turn to the answers.

Can you make the butterfly land on the flower?
See if you can do it, then turn to the answers to find out how.

Can you make the bulb light up?
The answers will tell you how.

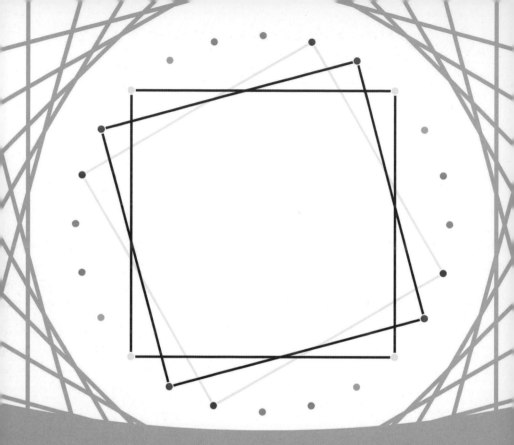

Using a black pen and a ruler, draw squares linking each set of dots. (The first two have been done for you.) What do you see when you've finished? See the answers for more about this.

Look at the cover of the blue book and the cover of the green one. They seem to be very different sizes and shapes. But are they really? Turn to the answers for a big surprise!

Move your eyes around this grid.
Are the lines wobbly or straight?
Find out in the answers section.

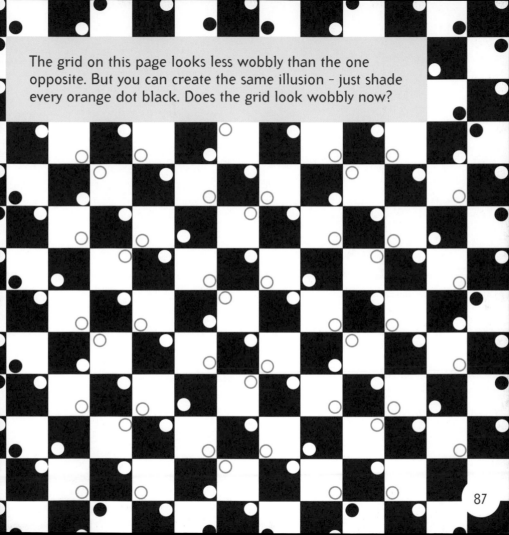

The grid on this page looks less wobbly than the one opposite. But you can create the same illusion – just shade every orange dot black. Does the grid look wobbly now?

87

Look carefully at the picture below, and remember exactly where the three glasses are. Now look at the picture on the opposite page.

Are the three glasses in different positions in this picture?
Are you sure? Turn to the answers to find out.

Move your eyes around this image.
Does it seem to be spinning around?

Is the person at the top of this page slightly taller than the one at the bottom? The answers will tell you.

Look at the pale orange diamonds on
this page, then look at the orange
diamonds on the opposite page.
Are the ones opposite darker?
Turn to the answers to
find out the truth.

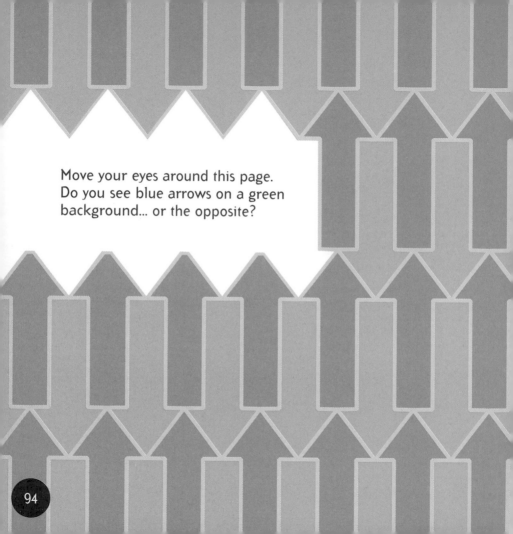

Move your eyes around this page. Do you see blue arrows on a green background... or the opposite?

Create your own version of the illusion below by filling in the rest of the arrows in blue and green.

Look at the two squares that are circled.
They seem to be very different – but are
they really? The answers will tell you.

Does this image seem to spin around? Shade in the rest of the pink and blue to make the illusion even stronger.

Look at the two red lines. The height of the mug looks greater than the width of the saucer. But is it really? See the answers to find out.

Using a ruler, draw a straight, vertical line between each pair of dots. (The first one has been done for you.) Now look at the lines you've drawn. Are they slanting, or parallel? The answers will tell you.

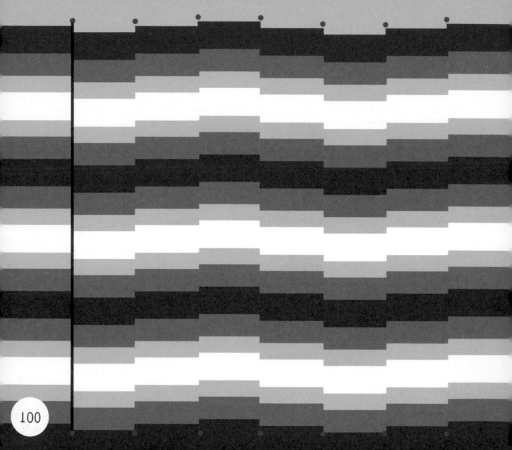

Are these lines bending and slanting, or are they completely straight? Find out in the answers section.

Shake this image gently left and right.
Can you see strange shapes swirling around the middle?

Is the castle on the right leaning more than the one on the left? Turn to the answers to find out.

Move the book gently up and down, and stare at the squares on this page. Does anything strange happen?

See the answers for more about this illusion.

Look at the two cats. Is Cat A taller than Cat B? Turn to the answers section to find out.

Do the squares on this page look as though they're slightly distorted and slanting? Or are they regular? The answers will tell you.

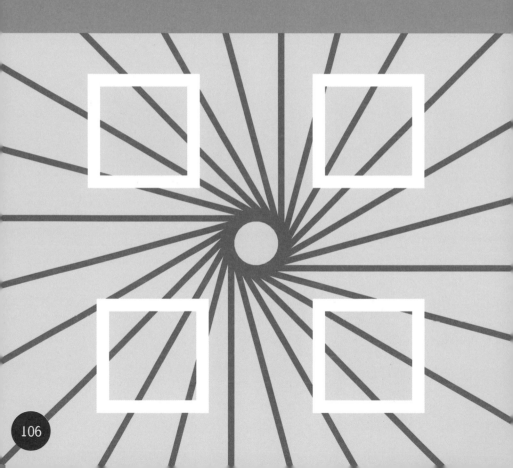

This square is completely regular. Using a ruler, join the dot in the middle to each dot around the edge. Does the square look slanted?

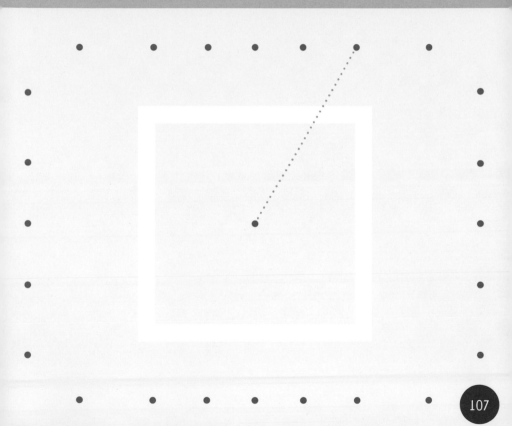

Look at the three orange waves. Is the middle one a darker orange than the other two? The answers will tell you.

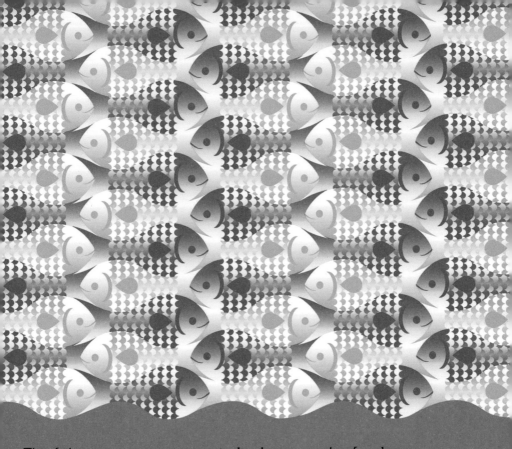

This fishy pattern contains vertical columns made of scales.
The columns seem to be tilting a lot to the left and right.
But are you sure that they really are? See the answers to find out.

110

Do the yellow, green and purple seem paler here? What happens if you shade the white areas black? See the answers to find out more.

Move your eyes around the page. What do you see? The answers will tell you more.

112

Look at the two octopuses. They seem to be very different shades of blue. But are they really? See the answers to find out.

2

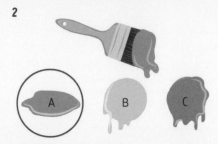

Surprisingly the answer is A, as you can see above. This illusion works because the shade of the background influences how we see the blue: when it's against a dark background it seems lighter, while a pale background makes it look darker.

3

Every line in the image is straight. The pattern of little squares confuses your mind, creating the effect of bendy lines.

4

All the rings are perfect circles, but the pattern of lines creates a powerful illusion that the circles are squashed out of shape.

7

All the red and yellow lines are straight and parallel. The pattern of little lines creates the illusion that they're tilting. Here you can see how the illusion vanishes when you remove those lines from part of the image.

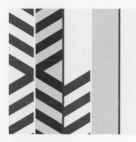

8-9

These two cubes show the two different ways you can view the pattern. You'll find that your eyes keep "flipping" from one of these ways of seeing it to the other.

10

Triangles A and F are exactly the same shade of blue, but it's almost impossible to see this because the different borders affect the way we see them.

The whole stripe below is the same shade – but notice how it seems to change because of what's around it.

12–13

Every line you drew on these pages is exactly the same length. There are many ways of fooling your eyes about the length of lines – here's a famous example.

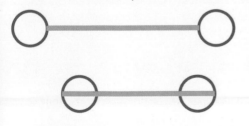

16–17

The two shapes in each pair are exactly the same size. As these two pages demonstrate, there are lots of different ways to trick your eyes about the size of things.

19

As you stare at the dot in the middle, the other dots will gradually fade until some of them disappear completely. If you stare for long enough, you might be able to make all the dots vanish.

20–21

This famous and very deceptive illusion was discovered by accident when a vision scientist happened to be staring at the wall of a café in Bristol, UK, and noticed that the parallel lines on the wall seemed to be tilting. It's now known as the Café Wall Illusion.

22

The orange stripes line up with each other perfectly, as you can see here. But it's very hard to see this when the angled lines are behind them.

23

All the circles are the same shade. But the different backgrounds and the lines across the circles create the illusion of different shades. If you remove the lines, the illusion is weaker, as you can see above.

27

Both pairs of semi-circles are exactly the same shade. If you remove everything else, like this, you can see this clearly.

29

The player could be kicking the ball towards us or away from us – it's impossible to say which, and you can make yourself see it both ways. If you add a few details, like this, you can make the player face away from you, or towards you.

30-31

All the shapes on these two pages are completely regular, but the lines behind them make them seem distorted. The squares below show how this works.

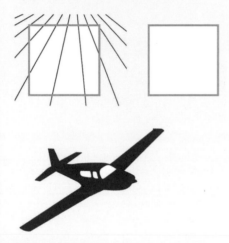

33

Here you can see what's hiding in the stripes – a plane. There are two ways of seeing it: either shake the page gently from side to side, or prop the book up on a table and look at the image from far away. Weirdly, it's easier to see the picture from far away than it is close-up.

34

The green and pink stripes are broken, as you can see below, but the blue one lines up perfectly even though it also seems to be broken. This powerful illusion was discovered in the 1800s.

36

If you stare directly at a black dot, it will vanish – since it's not really there! But if you move your eyes around again, you'll see the black dots at the edge of your vision. Many illusions work like this, creating effects not in what we're staring at but what we're glimpsing out of the corner of our eyes.

38

The yellow in stars A and B is identical, and so is the blue in stars C and D, as you can see here. The fuzzy outlines affect the way we see them, making two shades that are identical seem slightly different.

39

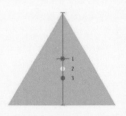

The correct answer is number 1, although most people think it's number 2. The triangle shape makes it very hard to judge the distances properly - because the top part is narrower we see that distance as shorter than it really is, while the bottom part of the triangle is much wider so that distance looks longer.

40

Both triangles are exactly the same shade throughout. The changing background creates the illusion that the triangles are much darker at one end - but as you can see below, this isn't true.

48

Amazingly, shapes A and B are exactly the same - the whole background of this page is the same shade of blue. To prove this to yourself, look at the image below. The little circles are darker in some areas than others, and this affects the way we see the background.

50

Both sets of arrows are exactly the same. If you remove the background like this, you can clearly see that they're identical.

51

When you see this image from far away, the stripes "mix" to create the illusion of one flat shade. This "blending" works in just the same way that it would if you were mixing paints: the red and yellow stripes look like orange, the red and blue ones make purple and the blue and yellow ones make green.

53

The secret to this illusion is to hold the book up to your eyes and tilt it away from you as much as you can while still seeing the image. Then close one eye... and you'll suddenly be seeing a flock of birds!

54

The first sentence should read:

What does this sentence mean?

Strangely, we're able to read this perfectly easily despite the fact that the letters in all the words are jumbled up. Our brains unscramble each group of letters and turn it into a word that we recognize.

54

Can you find a
(a)mistake in
(in)this sentence?

The second sentence contains two
mistakes, circled above. These are hard
to spot if you read it quickly, because
your mind combines both of the
repeated words into one.

It's quite easy to read this
sentence even with the bottom
half missing, isn't it?

55

Above is the first sentence, completed.
Most people find that it's surprisingly easy
to read text with the bottom half missing.
But this sentence, with the top half
missing, was probably harder for you:

But it's a little harder to read
something when the top half has
been taken away.

57

The whole background
is exactly the same
shade of pink, and it's
only the dark and light
stripes that make the
two halves of the page
seem different. This happens because our
brains blend the stripes with the pink. If
you remove the stripes from a section of
the image, like the bottom section of the
square above, the illusion vanishes.

60-61

When you stare at
the heart after looking
at the opposite page
for a long time, your
eyes "correct" the
heart image so that the whole thing looks
bright and the left-hand section no longer
appears to be in shadow. This illusion
works on the "after image" principle,
like the ones on pages 14-15 and 42-43:
your mind keeps "seeing" what you've
been staring at, and this affects how
you see the heart.

62–63

This well-known illusion relies on the fact that we still see a smile as a smile even if it's upside-down! Logically it should be obvious that the face on page 63 is frowning, but our brains tend to interpret it as a smiling face until we turn the page upside down.

64

Actually only one of the circles is squashed – the blue one. But the patterns and shapes around the other circles make all of them look slightly distorted. Here you can see how they look on a plain background.

65

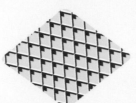

When you shake the book, the shape in the foreground should appear to move slightly against the background.

This illusion relies on the fact that the shape is in sharp focus and the background is fuzzy. If the background is clear, like this, the illusion vanishes.

68

All of the candy canes and lollipops are completely parallel. This simple but very deceptive illusion is created by the little angled lines along each one, and the wavy line along the bottom of the image. If you remove those elements, it's clear that they're all parallel.

Answers - pages 70 to 79

70

It's lots of separate circles - there's no spiral in this image. It's very hard not to see a spiral though, because the little black lines over the top of the circles confuse your eyes and make them jump from one circle to another. In the image on the right, with some lines removed, you can see what's happening.

71

The middle of the circles is exactly the same shade as the rings around them. The fuzzy edge on each ring makes it seem less bright, but as you can see here it's actually the same.

74-75

All the red in this image is exactly the same shade, and the same goes for the blue and the yellow. It looks as though there are lots of slightly different shades because of the way the red, yellow and blue are combined with each other and with black and white. Here you can see the same image with parts of it removed - it's easier to see now what's really happening.

78

All three shapes are exactly the same size.

79

All of the orange in this image is exactly the same shade, and the only reason we see it differently is the way the background

gradually changes. If you remove that background, the illusion completely disappears.

The rows of circles aren't tilting at all! This illusion is so strong that it's hard not to be fooled by it even when you know the truth. All that's tilting are the little lines on top of the circles – if you ignore those, then you can see that the rows of circles themselves are totally parallel.

82-83

To make the illusions on these two pages happen, just relax your eyes and stop focusing on the page until you start seeing two images at once. You'll find that you can make the

images move just by focusing a little less or a little more. Simply let the images move until you make the butterfly land on the flower and the bulb light up.

84

Did you end up with a circle? Surprising, isn't it, that you can make a circle without a single curved line? It's easy to create your own illusions like this, by drawing lots of straight lines with a ruler. Can you make a "wave" shape with only straight lines?

85

Incredibly, the two covers are exactly the same size and shape. This is one of the most powerful illusions ever invented and you'll probably need to measure each one before you believe it!

86

All the lines in the grid are straight and parallel. It's surprising how just adding a few black and white dots can fool our brains into seeing wobbly lines where none exist. You can see below how removing those dots makes the illusion disappear.

88-89

The three glasses are in exactly the same position in both pictures. All that's different is the position of the shadows beneath the glasses: on page 89 the shadows have been moved lower, which makes the glasses appear to be floating. But if you ignore the shadows and look at the glasses you'll see they haven't moved.

91

The two men are exactly the same height, but most people see the one at the top as slightly taller. This is because we know that the bottom person is "closer", and therefore we think he must actually be smaller than the top one.

92-93

The two sets of orange diamonds are exactly the same shade. As with the illusions on pages 2, 10 and 27, it's the background that influences the way we see them. Here's the same image without the background:

96-97

The two squares are exactly the same shade. This illusion works because part of the image seems to be in shadow and part of it is brightly lit. We see the square on page 96 as a pale square in shadow and the one on page 97 as a dark square with light shining on it. In reality, both are identical.

99

The height of the mug and the width of the saucer are identical, as you can see here. This simple, strong illusion is created partly by the fact that we tend to see vertical lines as longer than horizontal ones.

100

All the lines you've drawn are completely parallel. But the pattern around them makes it very hard to see it this way. Here's a section of the image with the

pattern removed, so you can see how the illusion vanishes without it:

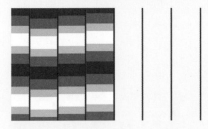

101

The lines are completely straight and parallel. The illusion is created by the little slanting lines on top of them, as you can see here.

103

The two castles are the same - the picture on the right is an exact duplicate of the one on the left, as you can see:

104

When you move the book, the little squares should appear to shake slightly and move in different directions. This happens because of the little black and white lines on the squares - without those lines, there's no illusion.

105

Both cats are exactly the same size. See the answer to page 91 for more about how this works.

106

All the squares are completely regular and their sides are parallel. The pattern of lines behind them creates the illusion that they're tilting and distorted.

108

All the orange in this image is the same shade, but the way we see it depends on what's around it - mingled with the blue squares it looks darker, and among the white squares it looks paler.

109

The columns of scales are all parallel. If you remove the rest of the pattern and just look at the columns, it's slightly easier to see this - though the illusion does remain.

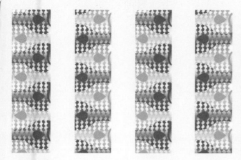

110-111

This illusion relies on the same kind of "blending" as the ones on pages 51 and 57: if we combine yellow with black, then it tends to look darker, and if we combine it with white, then it looks a little paler. Below you can see how this works.

112

When you move your eyes around this image, you'll see faint circles spreading out from the middle. These circles don't exist, but the pattern makes you "see" them.

113

The two octopuses are exactly the same. The shade of the water around them changes, and this is what makes us see them differently. Without the background water, the illusion vanishes.

Usborne Quicklinks

For links to websites where you can find out more about
optical illusions, and see lots more examples, go to the Usborne
Quicklinks website at **www.usborne.com/quicklinks** and enter
the keywords "pocket optical illusions". Please follow the internet
safety guidelines at the Usborne Quicklinks website.

First published in 2014 by Usborne Publishing Ltd., Usborne House, 83-85 Saffron
Hill, London EC1N 8RT, England. Copyright ©2014 Usborne Publishing Ltd.
The name Usborne and the devices 🎈🏺 are Trade Marks of Usborne Publishing
Ltd. All rights reserved. No part of this publication may be reproduced, stored
in a retrieval system, or transmitted in any form or by any means, electronic,
mechanical, photocopying, recording or otherwise without the prior permission
of the publisher. UE. Printed in Shenzhen, Guangdong, China.
First published in America in 2015.